Tear a loaf of bread, share a loaf of bread.
These Ethiopians are enjoying their bread together.

A thin pancake with sugar, washed down with tea.
Breakfast looks sweet in Iraq.

Big and tall or little and small – all these Afghan children love to eat bread.

Roll out the dough to make a poppadom. Indian women are rolling, rolling out the dough.

Let's all join in – everyone in Papua New Guinea
helps to make the meal.

In Burkina Faso they bake the bread in big, brown ovens.
Look at the lovely, long loaves.

Stretching out the noodles; long, stringy noodles.
The Chinese chef is making noodles for everybody's lunch.

Wash potatoes, scrub potatoes, peel potatoes and cook.
A Tajikistani family have potatoes for their lunch.

Cooking is easy if you know what to do. At school in Japan they find out just how to.

You can have lunch at school, and here in Japan it's healthy and tasty rice and salmon.

In a school in United Kingdom it's time for lunch, and it's time for friends – eating is more fun when friends are there too.

If the weather is hot like in Madagascar, school lunch is outside in long lines in the yard.

The classroom is also the lunchroom in this school in Congo. The children eat their food sitting at their desks.

Find something to eat and grab a seat – wherever that might be. These Chinese boys enjoy their corn sitting on the street.

In China, restaurants can pop up in the street
– a table and a cooking pot is all you need to rustle up a treat.

Having a picnic is lots of fun. In Japan these people have their lunch in the sun.

It's picnic time in India as well. These workers
take a break to have a bite to eat.

Some foods are just easier with a little help. In Argentina a grandpa holds the cup so a boy can suck up his drink.

In **Mongolia** too a mother feeds her daughter
– careful not to spill it!

Lovely juicy watermelon on a hot, sticky day – this European boy thinks there's nothing more refreshing!

While in Japan, crushed ice mixed with juice keeps this young girl cool.

Platefuls of perfect pasta are on the menu in France.
Sucking up spaghetti is fun but it can be messy!

In Taiwan they eat with chopsticks; two thin and fiddly sticks. But with a little practice even noodles are no problem.

Some food just needs to be eaten with your hands –
and these Chinese boys find their food is fun to eat.

In **Morocco** a great big bowl of meat and vegetables is a meal for all the family.

Something sweet is nice to eat. These Berbers have baked some Moroccan cakes – and there's enough for everyone.